my first rhyming picture abc

Written by Brian Miles.
Illustrated by Anne & Ken McKie.
Text © Brian Miles, 1985.
Illustrations © Grandreams Limited, 1985.

This edition published 1992.

Grandreams
Children's Book Publishers

Published by
GRANDREAMS LIMITED
Jadwin House, 205/211 Kentish Town Road, London, NW5 2JU.

Printed in Italy.   RB1-2

A a

a is for apples
some green, some red

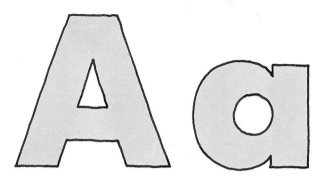

a is for aeroplane
that flies overhead

a is for apricot
that grows on a tree

a is for adding
one, two, three

B b

b is for baker
who bakes crusty bread

b is for blanket
that covers your bed

b is for beaker
for drinking your tea

b is for binoculars
for miles you can see

C c

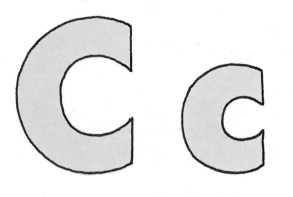

C is for cat
with its whiskers long

C is for cart
pulled by a horse so strong

C is for carrot
crunchy and sweet

C is for cars
that you see in the street

D d

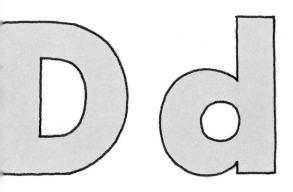

d is for dancing
so light on your feet

d is for drinking
orange juice so sweet

d is for dog
wagging his tail

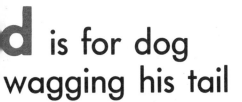

d is for dinghy
with a bright blue sail

E e

e is for eggs
see the chicks that hatch out

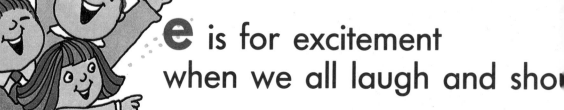

e is for excitement
when we all laugh and shou[t]

e is for elephant
so gentle but strong

e is for ending
the show with a son[g]

F f

f is for farm
with fresh milk and cheese

f is for fingers
the toothpaste to squeeze

f is for fan
a cool breeze to make

f is for fish
that swim in the lake

G g

g is for grapes
some green, some black

g is for garbage
that's put in a sack

g is for garden
where flowers do grow

g is for gumboots
to wear in the snow

H h

h is for hedgehog
who cleans up the garden

h is for hiccup
I beg your pardon!

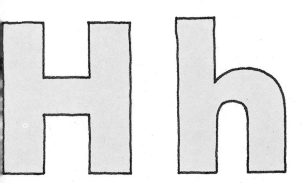

h is for hymn
that is sung in a church

h is for hen
asleep on her perch

Ii

i is for island
surrounded by sea

i is for iguana
a lizard you see

i is for inn
a welcoming sight

The Sun

i is for ivory
so smooth and so white

J j

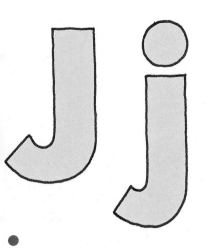

j is for jug
full of water so cool

J is for jumping
into the pool

j is for jam
to spread on your bread

STRAWBERRY JAM

J is for jet
that roars overhead

K k

k is for king
so stately and tall

k is for kitten
who plays with the ball

k is for kitchen
where cooking is done

k is for keeping
a secret, it's fun

L l

l is for lion
so noble and strong

l is for the lark
and merry birdsong

l is for leopard
known for his spots

l is for lemon
to squeeze lots and lots

M m

m is for mouse
who lives in a barn

m is for minstrel
who sings his own yarn

m is for mask
that hides your face

25miles

m is for marathon
a very long race

N n

n is for nurse
so patient with care

n is for nightingale
with its song so rare

n is for nut
so crunchy to eat

n is for navy
and ships in the fleet

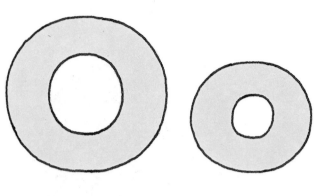

O is for orange
as round as a ball

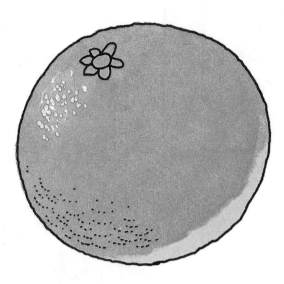

O is for ostrich
with its neck so tall

O is for oblong
longer than a square

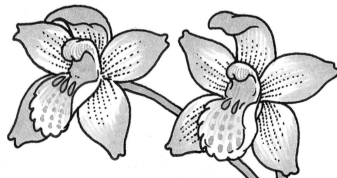

O is for orchid
a flower so rare

P p

p is for parrot
a beautiful bird

p is for pasture
and grazing a herd

p is for parachute
that floats to the ground

p is for pumpkin
oval or round

Qq

q is for quack
it's the way a duck talks

q is for queen
who smiles as she wal

q is for quilt
so warm yet so ligh

q is for quail
in migratory flight

R r

r is for robin
with its bright red breast

r is for rook
high in his nest

r is for roses
that grow down the lane

r is for rainbow
after the rain

S s

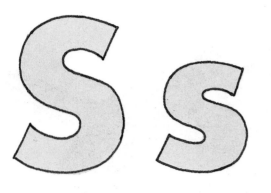

S is for sparrow
to the garden he comes

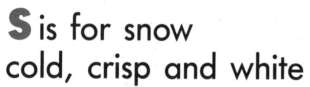

S is for starling
looking for crumb

S is for snow
cold, crisp and white

S is for stars
that shine in the nigh

T t

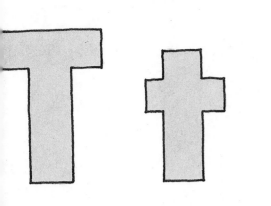

t is for target
at which we take aim

t is for teddybear
he's good for a game

t is for ticket
to ride on the train

t is for tea-time
it's jelly again!

U u

U is for universe
the planets and stars

U is for Uranus
a planet, like Mars

U is for uniforms
the guards in a row

U is for under
the arches we go!

Vv

V is for vine
heavy with fruit

V is for valet
preparing a suit

V is for vikings
who sailed the high seas

V is for vegetables
potatoes, parsnips and peas

Ww

W is for water
we use to make tea

W is for whale
that swims in the se

W is for the willow
that grows by the strear

W is for waking
from a beautiful dream

X x

X is for x-rays
used in hospitals you know
they can see through you
from your head to your toe

X is for xylophone
an instrument to play

X is for ten
the old roman way

Y y

y is for yellow
and daffodils so pale

y is for yacht
under full sail

y is for yeast
that helps make bread dough

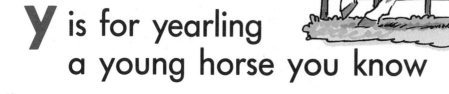

y is for yearling
a young horse you know

Z z

Z is for zebras
with their black and white coats

Z is for zither
playing musical notes

Z is for zoo
and the animals there

Z is for zig-zag
in a car beware

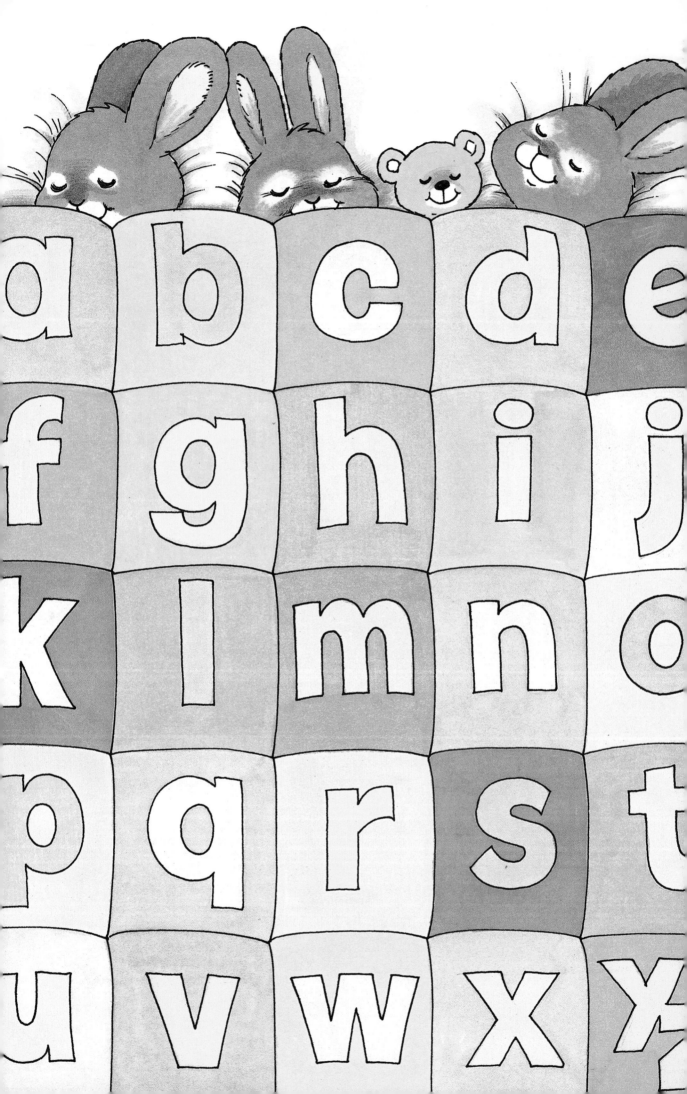